Visvavatan: 100 Demilitarization Sonnets

Abhijit Naskar is the 21st century Neuroscientist and Poet who has been serving at the forefront of humankind's struggle against hate, intolerance. bigotry and fanaticism.

Visvavatan

100 Demilitarization Sonnets

ABHIJIT
NASKAR

Also by Abhijit Naskar

The Art of Neuroscience in Everything
Your Own Neuron: A Tour of Your Psychic Brain
The God Parasite: Revelation of Neuroscience
The Spirituality Engine
Love Sutra: The Neuroscientific Manual of Love
Homo: A Brief History of Consciousness
Neurosutra: The Abhijit Naskar Collection
Autobiography of God: Biopsy of A Cognitive Reality
Biopsy of Religions: Neuroanalysis towards Universal
Tolerance
Prescription: Treating India's Soul
What is Mind?
In Search of Divinity: Journey to The Kingdom of Conscience
Love, God & Neurons: Memoir of a scientist who found
himself by getting lost
The Islamophobic Civilization: Voyage of Acceptance
Neurons of Jesus: Mind of A Teacher, Spouse & Thinker
Neurons, Oxygen & Nanak
The Education Decree
Principia Humanitas
The Krishna Cancer
Rowdy Buddha: The First Sapiens
We Are All Black: A Treatise on Racism
The Bengal Tigress: A Treatise on Gender Equality
Either Civilized or Phobic: A Treatise on Homosexuality
Wise Mating: A Treatise on Monogamy
Illusion of Religion: A Treatise on Religious
Fundamentalism
The Film Testament
Human Making is Our Mission: A Treatise on Parenting
I Am The Thread: My Mission
7 Billion Gods: Humans Above All
Lord is My Sheep: Gospel of Human
Morality Absolute
A Push in Perception
Let The Poor Be Your God
Conscience over Nonsense
Saint of The Sapiens
Time to Save Medicine

Fabric of Humanity
Build Bridges not Walls: In the name of Americana
The Constitution of The United Peoples of Earth
Lives to Serve Before I Sleep
When Humans Unite: Making A World Without Borders
All For Acceptance
Monk Meets World
Mission Reality
Citizens of Peace: Beyond The Savagery of Sovereignty
Operation Justice: To Make A Society That Needs No Law
See No Gender
The Gospel of Technology
Every Generation Needs Caretakers: The Gospel of
Patriotism
Aşkanjali: The Sufi Sermon
Mad About Humans: World Maker's Almanac
Revolution Indomable
When Call The People: My World My Responsibility
No Foreigner Only Family
Hurricane Humans: Give me accountability, I'll give you
peace
Ain't Enough to Look Human
Servitude is Sanctitude
Time To End Democracy: The Meritocratic Manifesto
I Vicdansaadet Speaking: No Rest Till The World is Lifted
Boldly Comes Justice: Sentient not Silent
Good Scientist: When Science and Service Combine
Sleepless for Society
Neden Türk: The Gospel of Secularism
Martyr Meets World: To Solve The Hard Problem of
Inhumanity
The Shape of A Human: Our America Their America
When Veins Ignite: Either Integration or Degradation
Heart Force One: Need No Gun to Defend Society
Solo Standing on Guard: Life Before Law
Generation Corazon: Nationalism is Terrorism
Mucize Insan: When The World is Family
Hometown Human: To Live For Soil and Society
Girl Over God: The Novel (Abi Naskar Adventures Book 1)
Gente Mente Adelante: Prejudice Conquered is World
Conquered
Earthquakin' Egalitarian: I Die Everyday So Your Children
Can Live
Giants in Jeans: 100 Sonnets of United Earth

Vatican Virus: The Forbidden Fiction (Abi Naskar
Adventures Book 2)
Karadeniz Chronicle: The Novel (Abi Naskar Adventures
Book 3)
Şehit Sevda Society: Even in Death I Shall Live
Handcrafted Humanity: 100 Sonnets For A Blunderful
World
Mücadele Muhabbet: Gospel of An Unarmed Soldier
Making Britain Civilized: How to Gain Readmission to The
Human Race
Dervish Advaitam: Gospel of Sacred Feminines and Holy
Fathers
Honor He Wrote: 100 Sonnets For Humans Not Vegetables
The Gentalist: There's No Social Work, Only Family Work
Either Reformist or Terrorist: If You Are Terror I Am Your
Grandfather
Woman Over World: The Novel (Abi Naskar Adventures
Book 4)
High Voltage Habib: Gospel of Undoctrination
Bulldozer on Duty
Find A Cause Outside Yourself: Sermon of Sustainability
Ingan Impossible: Handbook of Hatebusting
Amor Apocalypse: Canım Sana İhtiyacım
Amantes Assemble: 100 Sonnets of Servant Sultans
Mucize Misafir Merhaba: The Peace Testament
Divane Dynamite: Only truth in the cosmos is love
Sin Dios Sí Hay Divinidad: The Pastor Who Never Was
Corazon Calamidad: Obedient to None, Oppressive to None
Esperanza Impossible: 100 Sonnets of Ethics, Engineering &
Existence
Mukemmel Musalman: Kafir Biraz, Peygamber Biraz
Himalayan Sonneteer: 100 Sonnets of Unsubmission
Yarasistan: My Wounds, My Crown
The Centurion Sermon: Mental Por El Mundo
Her Insan Ailem: Everyone is Family, Everywhere is Home
Humankind, My Valentine: World's First Anthology of 1000
Sonnets
Aşk Mafia: Armor of The World
Vande Vasudhaivam: 100 Sonnets for Our Planetary Pueblo
Visvavictor: Kanima Akiyor Kainat
Sapionova: 200 Limericks for Students
Rowdy Scientist: Handbook of Humanitarian Science
Insan Himalayanoğlu: It's Time to Defect

Tum Dunya Tek Millet: Greatest Country on Earth is Earth
Either Right or Human: 300 Limericks of Inclusion

Yaralardan Yangın Doğar: Explorers of Night are Emperors
of Dawn
Bulletproof Backbone: Injustice Not Allowed on My Watch
Poesía Humanitaria: Cien Sonetos Para Mi Familia Mundial
(Spanish)
Iman Insaniyat, Mazhab Muhabbat: Pani, Agua, Water, It's
All One
Yüz Şiirlerin Yüzüğü (Turkish)

DEDICATION

To my homeworld – earth.

CONTENTS

1.   Letter to My Soldiers

Letter to My Soldiers

I am only the beginning - the beginning of a new kind of humans - humans who belong to not one culture, but many cultures - humans who speak not one language, but many languages - humans who study scriptures and science with equal enthusiasm, yet pledge allegiance to neither, and know how to use both in the benefit of humanity - humans who aim for neither belief nor disbelief, but warmth and understanding - humans who are more concerned with the real hard problem of inhumanity, than the outdated hard problem of consciousness - humans who sacrifice their life treating the real hard question of hate, rather than the mythical hard question of god. I am only the beginning - the first spark, if you may - the best are yet to come.

Carta a Mis Soldados

Soy sólo el comienzo – el comienzo de nuevos humanos – humanos que pertenecen no a una cultura, sino a muchas culturas – humanos que hablan no un idioma, sino muchos idiomas –

humanos que estudian las escrituras y la ciencia con igual entusiasmo, pero que no juran lealtad a ninguna de las dos, y saben cómo usar ambas en beneficio de la humanidad - humanos que no buscan ni la creencia ni la incredulidad, sino la calidez y la comprensión - humanos que están más preocupados por el problema realmente difícil de la inhumanidad que por el anticuado problema de la conciencia - humanos que sacrifican su vida resolviendo la cuestión primitiva del odio, en lugar de la cuestión mítica de dios. Soy sólo el comienzo - puedes decir, el primer fuego - lo mejor está por llegar.

I repeat.
I am only the first fire,
the best are yet to come!

2.   Hands (Sonnet 1301)

World First, Nation Never
(Denationalizing Sonnet, 1301)

No government wants to manufacture terror,
But they do want to manufacture control.
In doing so they end up manufacturing terror,
Thus they end up manufacturing war.

There is no such thing as war on terrorism,
The whole narrative is rigged to peddle fear.
Citizens without fear are citizens without border,
Democratic autocracy thrives on civilian fear.

Ceasefire only postpones war,
What's needed is demilitarization.
Till borderly apes wake apart national pride,
Democracy only sustains a paradigm of poison.

World first and forever, nation never;
Till then, all blood is on your hands.
Either you are a nation's simian citizen,
or you are planet earth's civilized human.

3.   Orphanizers (Sonnet 1302 - 1304)

Sonnet 1302

Denationalization is civilization,
Demilitarization is only peacemaking.
Warmongers gotta peddle war no matter what,
Why do beings with backbone keep submitting!

They say, a nation is as strong as its military.
I say, a nation is as stupid as its warmongers.
It takes very little to defend a nation,
But all the arsenal won't satisfy warmakers.

Give me a team of five, with an engineer,
physicist, mathematician, coder and composer,
And I'll improvise a nation impenetrable,
without needing to kill a single soldier.

Defense of the nation is not the problem,
Real question is, whom are you defending against?
How long will you entertain prehistoric paranoia,
When will you grow out of all defense and offense?

Orphanizers
(Demilitarization Sonnet, 1303)

Show me a nation with a huge defense budget,
I'll show you a demented nation.
Show me a nation with a big education budget,
I'll show you a nation of the future.

Disband the soldiers, empower the teachers,
Thus you plant the paradigm of peace.
Abolish all pride in nation's military,
Thus you emerge as maker of peace.

The real warmongers of the world are,
Not the world leaders, but the civilians,
Who can't think past the strength of military,
Who take pride in a genocidal arsenal of weapons.

With such civilian primitiveness rampant in society,
No conference can ensure the promise of peace.
If you really want to ensure peace on planet earth,
Denounce all politics and democracy militarist.

Stop taking pride in your national military,
That very pride floods the world with orphans.
Amidst the herd of widowmakers and orphanizers,
Wake up alone, and slogan for demilitarization!

Pro Government or Pro Human Rights
(Earth Administrative Service, Sonnet 1304)

Either pro government or pro human rights,
A civilized human cannot be both.
Doesn't mean you're always anti government,
It means you pledge no one blanket support.

Gaza has made it more evident than ever,
No politician got the guts to rock the boat.
When the chips are down and balloon goes up,
Politicians hide behind the diplomacy door.

World leeches masquerading as world leaders,
Would sell their mothers if the price is right.
Sheeply civilians don't do much to change things,
So they seek comfort in snobbish arguments on AI.

Dump all autocratic nonsense of law-abidance,
Tell the right from wrong by conscience rule.
If you want human rights to reign supreme,
Wake up and be the world leader of your hood.

4. Administration
(Sonnet 1305 - 1307)

Earth Administrative Service, Sonnet 1305

Run for service, not office.
Chase change, not campaign victory.
If you can't change the world without office,
    you definitely can't change it in office.

Who am I? I am Abhijit Naskar, EAS -
Earth Administrative Servant the First.
Who's next - who is thunderful enough,
    to shoulder the world as living Atlas!

Politicians are like dumb nuclear weapons,
    it feels good to have some,
    but in the end they achieve nothing,
while all the tasks are actually accomplished
    by regular civilians and civil servants.

Representative democracy is an outdated concept,
    Particularly the concept of government.
If you really wanna end politics from society,
You gotta end the very concept of government.

Earth Administrative Service, Sonnet 1306

Doctors are not official representatives,
Yet they do their job quite efficiently.
Teachers are not official representatives,
Yet they do their job quite respectfully.

Public transport drivers ain't representatives,
Yet they carry their duties quite diligently.
Factory workers ain't official representatives,
Yet they fulfill their tasks rather honorably.

All the professions that actually require
some tangible skillsets and expertise,
don't rely on the jungle whim of democracy.
Yet the most glorified profession of all,
has no performance standards compulsory.

If this is your idea of a civilized democracy,
No wonder you still crave peace in nuclear weapons!
Only monkeys could confuse homicide with defense,
It takes a human to plant peace through illumination.

Boycott Taxes, Boycott War
(Demilitarization Sonnet, 1307)

When animals pick up weapons, it's jungle necessity.
When humans pick up weapons, it is social stupidity.
If weapons are still your default mode of security,
Yours is another animal kingdom, not human society.

You spend a fraction of your budget on disinfectant,
Yet your government spends most on defense equipment.
How could you submit to such prehistoric atrocity,
Let alone take pride in such savage derangement!

Boycott all government till they ban all military,
Don't pay taxes till they declare permanent ceasefire.
When one person fails to file taxes, it is tax fraud.
When the planet boycotts taxes, it is law of nature.

Let all governments know, absolute submission is obsolete.
They exist so long as they serve the interest of humanity.
The moment they are up to their old apish tricks,
No amount of curfew will save their seat of atrocity.

5.   White Crimes
(Sonnet 1308 - 1310)

White Fragility Sonnet, 1308
(A Record of White Crimes Against Humanity)

Whiteness has done more harm to the world than good,
Till you look past your whiteness, you cannot be human.
Orange 'n musky trash of white privilege diss diversity,
What else would you expect from colonial descendants!

Every generation has its fraudsters like Edison,
Every generation has trashy maniacs like Columbus.
Every generation has war-merchants like Kissinger,
Every generation has its churchillian doofus.

White people tortured the Africans,
White people booted Native Americans;
White people massacred the Vietnamese,
White people lynched and looted the Indians.

White people caused genocide after genocide,
Yet you still boast about white superiority.
You proclaim that people of color are inferior,
While white society is the epitome of savagery.

White Fragility Sonnet, 1309

If devil had a color, it would be white -
Yet I say, color is nonsense, we're all equal.
I am human enough to give you place beside me,
All I expect is that, a human behaves human.

After all the heartaches inflicted by white people,
A 100 generations worth apology won't be sufficient.
Yet I am human enough to declare, we are all equal;
All I ask is that, humans finally behave human.

They say, I'm spreading hate against the whites;
To which I say, human making is my mission.
There is no hope for humanitarian uplift,
Unless you renounce all fragile intoleration.

If you wanna learn about tolerance, ask a person of color,
How do you even tolerate the sight of white people, when
the wrongs done to you by whites are unparalleled in history!
You'll realize, there's no mythical secret to integration,
For ages we've known no other life but of inclusivity.

White Fragility Sonnet, 1310

Middle East, India and Far East,
have been the melting pot of integration,
before the whites even knew what integration is.
Yet you say white people are superior - so be it;
Cowards always take refuge in fairytales,
to justify their fragility and prejudice.

If you wanna be a decent human being,
Never draw moral parameters from the west.
No matter whether you're born of east or west,
Remember, you are human first, then all else.

To recognize diversity is science,
To celebrate diversity is humanity.
To recognize privilege is common sense,
To abandon privilege builds human society.

Note: In hollywood white man saves the world, in the real world white man has wrecked the world more times than he could make amends for in a thousand years.

So, to get straight to the point - the only way America could be considered a civilized nation, is if we embrace and celebrate our identity as an integrated society - otherwise, everything about America screams savagery.

The same holds true for England, as well as France, Spain and Portugal. Every society born of colonial roots, must abandon the garbage geopolitical dream of becoming a superpower, and place all their attention on making amends for the past - at least until prejudice and discrimination are no longer a dominant force in these societies. It's not about feeling guilty, it's about feeling human, and doing everything it takes to correct the mistakes that keep you from becoming human. And for that, it is imperative, you abandon your make believe glories of the past and look at the world with human eyes. Or to put it plainer still - it's not your fault that your ancestors were jerks, but if you fail to right their wrongs as civilized human, then you are just as jerk as them.

Let me put this into perspective with the simple example of Christmas. You celebrate Christmas as the occasion of the birth of a child, yet your very ancestry is rooted in a paradigm that till this day makes orphans out of children religiously. Your ancestors called it "march of civilization" - your modern political overlords call it "national defense". Now do you see the fallacy of your so-called glory!

If you cared about the thousands of children suffering today in Gaza, as much you care about the birth of one middle eastern child two thousand years ago, perhaps then, you could've understood the true meaning of Christmas.

As of now, Christmas is just a festival of hypocrisy - and that too, in the name of a man who gave his life to lift up the fallen. My question is, if you cannot be Christlike in your deeds, what's the point of all these festivities, which are supposed to be rooted in goodwill towards all, not mindless self-obsession!

6.   National Hero
(Sonnet 1311 - 1313)

World Gospel
(The Sonnet, 1311)

So long as there is selfishness,
There is no Christmas.
So long as there is occupation,
There is no Hanukkah.
So long as there is cruelty,
There is no Ramadan.
Till we end militant atheism,
There is no Humanism.
Till you conquer superstition,
There is no Diwali.
So long as there is division,
There is no Vaisakhi.
So long as there is inequality,
There is no Fourth of July.
Till we abolish hate from earth,
At half mast all flags must fly.

Note: Militant atheism is the antithesis of humanism. Fundamentalism is the antithesis of religion. Nationalism is the antithesis of peace.

I am Multiculturalism
(The Sonnet, 1312)

I don't write on multiculturalism,
I am multiculturalism.
The only nationalism I care about,
is tribalism ending multinationalism.

I can't do it no more - I can't!
One little language is enough no more!
I gotta be the Himalayas in every language,
I gotta be the Himalayas in every culture.

Either you'll know me as a national hero
of every nation, or you won't know me at all.
So long as a single human calls me foreigner,
I'll conclude, I've achieved nothing at all.

There is no stranger, only neighbor.
Everyone is family, no one is foreigner.

(No hay extraño, sólo vecino.
Todos familia, no hay extranjero.)

One Mission, Many Vessels
(The Sonnet, 1313)

One thunder, visions plenty.
One mission, vessels plenty.
One source, seekers plenty.
One fate, fervors plenty.

From dust we're born,
In dust we're gone.
Cashes to ashes,
Bitcoins in trashes,
Division is nefarious,
Unity is dawn.

The day the billions of people of earth
are valued more than the billionaires,
that day you shall be human being,
that day you are king and queen.

Naskar doesn't have flag or nation,
My flag is world flag - my nation, world nation.
Call me poet, scientist or humanitarian,
Naskar is the spirit of world integration.

7.   Duty (Sonnet 1314 - 1316)

Sonnet 1314

Be ready at heart,
Brain and backbone will follow.
Be ready with tenacity,
Path and sight will follow.

Be ready with intention,
Illumination will follow.
Be ready with determination,
Dynamism will follow.

Be ready with heartwashed soul,
Godlike conviction will follow.
Stand primed by self-annihilation,
Blunder-treating thunder will follow.

Tranquility lies in every atom,
Every atom holds apocalypse.
Light is intrinsic to every atom,
Every atom is volcanic.

Note: The biggest requirement of learning is to know your limits of the moment. Let me elaborate with an example. Alongside my mainstream works, I have wanted to create complete works in turkish and spanish for several years. And few years back, with my rather limited experiential understanding of both languages, I even took it upon myself to do so, but I got stuck on the very first page. Why? Because it is one thing to pen occasional gems in another language, and totally different to release an entire work in that language. I was ready at heart, but not at brain. So, instead of writing whole works in these languages, I simply made turkish and spanish a joyful addition to my mainstream work - however the original linguistic and cultural intention kept reflecting in the titles of works, such as Aşkanjali, The Gentalist, Gente Mente Adelante, Mucize Insan and so on. It was not until late 2023 that my brain finally caught up with my heart, and delivered the first complete original turkish and spanish Naskarean works to the world.

Know your strongholds, they'll take you far. Know your shortfalls, they'll take you farther. Strongholds help you enhance your predominant capacities, whereas shortfalls help you unfold new possibilities - they help you unfold new vistas of human endeavor.

Dutybound, Sonnet 1315

To treat disease you need medical license,
To treat injustice being human is enough.
To fly a plane you need pilot's license,
To lift up society being human is enough.

To talk to computers you gotta learn coding,
To listen to people being human is enough.
To build a shuttle you need rocket science,
To build a society being human is enough.

To analyze behavior study neuropsychology,
To accept people being human is enough.
To practice law you gotta pass the Bar exam,
To practice humanity being human is enough.

To make it rain on land in drought,
you gotta seed the clouds with dry ice.
To make it rain on hearts in drought,
just lend a hand, and smile without price.

Sonnet 1316

Society is not a stock market,
where the supreme measure is money.
One smile, one hug, is worth more,
than all the dough in US treasury.

Currency fluctuates based on geography,
A smile is worth the same wherever you go.
Now tell me what is more valuable,
One gentle smile or a pocket full of dough!

Real value of currency and clothes,
are delivered by their bearer.
Underneath the clothes if chest is vacant,
no currency can help build character.

For a well built character currency is tool,
For apes without character currency is god.
For a well built character code is tool,
For apes without heart code is god.

8.   Shall Meet
(Sonnet 1317 - 1319)

Code War
(Sonnet 1317)

The next world war is
not gonna be a cold war,
it's gonna be a code war.
Forget about conscious AI,
ethicless AI is the real danger.

Codes don't have to be conscious,
to do great damage to the world.
ChatGPT, Deepfake, Dall-E, none
are sentient, yet there is no limit
to them-produced fraud and havoc.

Without a basic righteousness code,
Fanciest of algorithm is mindless junk.
If you cannot figure out how to do that,
Abandon digital and build back analog.

Focus on ethical AI, rather than smarter AI,
If you are human, and wanna help the world.
If you're a robot who thinks logic is king,
Get yourself admitted, for you are in muck.

Sonnet 1318

Code age is the new ice age,
Where logic undermines warmth.
If this is your idea of progress,
Silicon chips are glorified junk.

From jungle roots to silicon chips,
Absence of conscience turns all to chains.
Bow and arrows to nuclear weapons,
Tech may differ, primitivity is the same.

We brought the moon to our doorstep,
Yet nextdoor neighbors remain ever distant.
What's the point of sailing to Mars, when
the minds at flight deck are same old unsapient!

Soon moon will become a tourist spot,
Rich kids will travel to have fun,
While people on earth keep suffering,
As they have been eon after eon.

Shall Meet You There
(Sonnet 1319)

Beyond tongue and tradition,
Beyond king and nation,
Beyond ignorance and intolerance,
Beyond cowardice and castration,
Beyond fear and fanaticism,
Beyond rigidity and recklessness,
Beyond the desert of dead habit,
Beyond the logical heartlessness,
Beyond the guise of practicality,
Beyond the price of convenience,
Beyond the lies of selfish order,
Beyond the highs of whims and wishes,
There's a valley of love and laughter.
Come someday, I shall meet you there.

9. Greed (Sonnet 1320 - 1322)

Smoking is Good
(Sonnet Satire, 1320)

Smoking is good for the planet,
For it screws with the lungs.
Alcohol is good for the planet,
For it screws with the brain.
Bullets are good for the planet,
They riddle the body with holes.
Bombs are good for the planet,
They blow up all, body and soul.
Autocracies are good for the planet,
They cause civilizations to fall.
Mindless tech is good for the planet,
Our biggest wonder will be our downfall.
Whatever kills the humans, heals the planet.
Forget AI, human greed is the biggest threat.

Sonnet 1321

For the humans to be a boon to the planet,
like the planet has been to the humans,
we humans gotta put an end to our greed,
we gotta abandon all self-obsession.
Until we consciously grab hold of our greed,
We are nothing but worthless dust makers.
Everything we touch turns to dust,
We are nothing but intelligent vultures.
Greed makes us narrow,
Greed shrinks our soul.
Beyond greed lies gallantry,
Beyond greed all is whole.
Narrow mind leads to vacant marrow,
Without expansion life is hollow.

Sonnet 1322

Walls deserve zero respect,
Walls are but illusion.
Ceilings deserve zero allegiance,
Ceilings are but delusion.
There is light beyond the wall,
There is sky beyond the ceiling.
Walls broken is world awakened,
Ceiling breaking is sky awakening.
Bring down the ceiling,
Break down the walls.
Anything dividing mind from mind,
Refute them boldly and go awol.
It's good to tolerate little fiction,
not walls, ceilings, and such primitivity.
It's more important to tell good fiction
from bad, than to tell fiction from reality.

10. The Giant (Sonnet 1323 - 1325)

Sonnet 1323

All reality is fiction,
All fiction is reality.
Our choice unfolds our reality,
Destiny is an act of duty.

Zero and infinity are one and the same,
Every zero contains the infinity.
Zero and hero are one and the same,
Every zero hides within heroic bravery.

Duty and destiny are one and the same,
Choose your duty, destiny gains in sight.
Mission and mind are one and the same,
Discovery of mission is discovery of mind.

Let no tradition come between you and your dream.
Better abandon citizenship than abandon your dream.

Hometown Giant
(Sonnet 1324)

A civilized world is not where everybody
flocks to another nation to fulfill their dream,
but where everybody can pursue their dream
without feeling the need to become an immigrant.

For years I got knocked about by bureaucrats
and politicians of a stoneage state.
So I cut off all national attachment
and focused all my powers on the west.

Only after the west recognized me as an icon,
I was able to unfold my vision worldwide.
The world is filled with such hometown giants,
Who find it impossible to keep hope alive.

A genius doesn't need the state,
It's the state that needs the genius.
When you lose a genius to another nation,
You push your country backwards a hundred years.

Sonnet 1325

This is my word to the states of earth,
Try to get it through your thick head.
If your top export is not merchandise
but immigrants, know that you've failed.

The very concept of state is stoneage,
But since it exists it must elevate life.
As of now, some states empower genius,
While jerks ridicule the dreamer life.

Any donkey can recognize a bright light,
It takes humans to fuel the light in making.
Hence all they do is mock dream pursuit,
Since underneath their skin they're all vermin.

Forget government and work on your dream,
In time governments will flock at your door.
Civilization is shaped by dreams,
not by government floor.

11. Stateless (Sonnet 1326 - 1328)

Stateless Sonnet, 1326

Some dreams are too big for a town,
Some dreams are too big for a city.
My dream was too big for one country,
So I stood up and engulfed humanity.

I am too alive to be bound by ideology,
I am too human to be bound by border.
Too civilized to pledge flagly allegiance,
I am the ultimate geopolitical defector.

In poetry I am sufi,
In philosophy I am advaitin.
In duty I am scientist,
In existence I am human.

I am a civilized human being,
I don't exist to impress governments.
I'm a being with heart, brain 'n backbone,
I'm the stateless force of world upliftment.

Sonnet 1327

Grow so big with your ideas that you become
a threat to every nationalist state in the world.
Grow so big with inclusivity that you become a curse
to every fundamentalist institution in the world.

Pledge allegiance to no label,
Be absolutely, unequivocally nondual.
Move past even the concept of nonduality,
So that you become unequivocally whole.

Nonduality or Advaita means that we gotta
renounce all things that create division,
including the very term "advaita",
as well as the label of nondualism.

Expand, expand, and expand again,
till the world witnesses your human reign.
Expand to serve, expand to love!
Amidst eternal desert be the impossible rain.

Sonnet 1328

All deserts are born of human coldness,
Humans must take the responsibility.
Crouch and chant all you want,
That won't make it rain on society.

Rainmaking is an act of love,
Rainmaking is an act of accountability.
Make believe may bring personal comfort,
It does nothing to elevate the community.

Community rises when consciousness rises,
Consciousness rises when conscience rises.
Conscience rises when oneness manifests,
Oneness manifests when love rises.

Desert outside is reflection
of the coldness inside.
Eliminate inner coldness,
and watch the drought subside!

12. Vacant (Sonnet 1329 - 1331)

Sonnet 1329

To fight is easy, but to create trust
where there is none, that's the real challenge.
To argue is easy, but to foster understanding
where there is none, that's the real challenge.

Tears speak the same tongue
wherever they are shed.
Smiles speak the same tongue
wherever they are cracked.

Neither tears nor smiles
discriminate between mind and mind,
then why do you encourage division,
why should a mind be separate from mind!

Diversity is an act of nature,
Inclusion is an act of mind.
Diversity is the presence of light,
Inclusion is the celebration of light.

Sonnet 1330

Everybody wants to rule the world,
That's why they never rule the world.
The only people to rule the world
are those who want only to serve the world.

Service is the supreme rule,
Service is the supreme wisdom.
No leader like servant leader,
In service there is union.

One more brain won't make much difference,
But one less heart makes all the difference.
Without the heartfelt duty of belonging,
Mightiest of brain ends up in ruin.

Might makes no difference,
without the sight of heart.
Might of brain is worthless,
without the mercy of heart.

Sonnet 1331

You cannot live in a multidimensional
world with a two-dimensional mind.
You cannot understand multidimensional
society with two-dimensional sight.

Stronger the mind,
gentler the mind.
Braver the mind,
humbler the mind.

While empty fleshbags mock the gentle,
Gentleness is the mark of strength.
While vacant egotists mock the humble,
Humility is the mark of substance.

End of self is the beginning of life.
Containing the world you rise to light.

13. Comatose (Sonnet 1332 - 1334)

Failing to be American
(The Sonnet, 1332)

I've tried to rekindle the American sentiment
of my early days of writing, but in vain.
Once you wake up to the vastness of the world,
it is impossible to revert to the tribal lane.

I broke into the world scene as a westerner but,
Naskar the American writer exists no longer.
Today Naskar is but an Earth philosopher,
There is only Naskar the Earth reformer.

In the early years when I wrote on America,
I used to write as an American writer.
Today when I write on any nation,
I write as an Earth writer.

The whole world is my diary,
I am the world's destiny.
Try as they might to maintain prejudice,
I am the line between humanity and nationality.

Sonnet 1333

It's a slippery slope from
nationality to nationalism.
More you obsess over nationality,
More you degrade into nationalism.

Keep your nationality if you wish,
But don't go crazy over it.
Keep your passport like bus pass,
And everything is well and dandy.

Your bus pass is not your identity,
It's just a useful tool for travel.
That's what your national ID is,
a piece of paper, somewhat tolerable.

What nationality is the sun!
What nationality is the moon!
No constitution contains the heavens,
Books bound to borders are no moral boon.

Sonnet 1334

Love is poetry of the cosmos,
Love is constitution supreme.
Breaking all comatose sanity,
Love dawns consciousness supreme.

Justice is just byproduct of love,
Equality is but byproduct of love.
In love there is no self, no other,
All are one, everything is love.

Borders are fiction,
Benevolence is real.
Law is fancy make believe,
Love alone is real.

Heart of love contains the world,
Such heart needs neither law nor faith.
Immeasurable love is measure supreme,
Second hand measures are of no consequence.

14. Prophet (Sonnet 1335 - 1337)

Sonnet 1335

Everything must be above board,
There is no room for deceit.
Acknowledge those who help you grow,
Fraudulence is mark of cowardice.

After my first few works I stopped citing
even my own old passages in new books.
Connected to their predecessors only by spirit,
I wanted new works to be unapologetically new.

I never grew up dreaming to be a writer,
I started to walk and the path appeared.
Only after I started writing quite on a whim,
that I realized the power I hold over words.

Some make cars,
Some make rockets.
I am reformer, not entrepreneur.
I make Gods and Prophets.

Sonnet 1336

Only a multicultural polyglot,
who has wiped out borders from heart,
rising above both intellect and faith,
can sense the immenseness of my work.

The immeasurable cannot be contained
by the measures of a sectarian core.
To experience the immeasurable ocean,
you must abandon your shorely allure.

Even reason is of no use,
if the heart is stuck behind wall.
No reason can make you see light,
unless the heart wakes up to the world.

Head without heart is dead,
Voice without vision is noise.
Body without backbone is carcass,
Consciousness without expansion is carnage.

Sonnet 1337

Our society, our sapling!
We gotta nurture it as prophet supreme.
Ain't no other prophet, no other god but us.
We are what we seek - whole world our kin.

Whole world is love sovereign,
Every lover is emperor.
Our planet, we are prophets,
Every person is peacemaker.

What the world needs is
spirituality without superstition.
What the world needs is
religion without discrimination.

Citizens beyond scripture
are citizens without fear.
Citizens beyond border
are world unifier.

15. Elemental (Sonnet 1338 - 1340)

Sonnet 1338

For justice I am mental,
My honor is not rental.
Amidst all heritage of fear,
I choose to be love elemental.

Ancient fiction writers used to say,
The universe is made of five elements.
I say, to hell with five elements,
All cosmos is contained in love element!

Only element I care about is love,
Only gospel I care about is love.
Only law I care about is love,
Only divinity I care about is love.

Only nationality I care about is love,
Only religion I care about is love.
No fiction, no fact, is higher
than the truth of love.

Sonnet 1339

Love elemental is more than sentimental,
In it unfolds existence universal.
Heart universal is beyond philosophical,
It is the gateway to peace unchainable.

Peace happens when you rise above prejudice,
World happens when you rise above nationality.
Holiness happens when you rise above scripture,
Humanity unfolds beyond cultural exclusivity.

Priority makes the person,
Person makes the world.
When the world is personal priority,
Civilization transcends library halls.

The library is worth more than the bank,
As a repository of human ascension.
But ascension trapped inside the library,
Is only ascension of mythical fiction.

Ascension must manifest in the individual,
That's true manifestation of civilization.
And civilization can never manifest so long
as you glorify your ancestral degradation.

Dedicated to Hitler
(Sonnet of Lesser Evil, 1340)

I'll write a book of german sonnets,
and dedicate it to Adolf Hitler.
The very thought makes you mad right!
I feel the same way when you
glorify Churchill as savior.

The west has systematically peddled
morons and monkeys as kings heroic,
white suffering is human suffering, while
the colored belong on national geographic.

Sure every society has its own troubles,
All of humanity has its inhumanity.
But the west doesn't have the high ground,
to pass judgment on ethics and morality.

If morality did have a scale,
West would be scraping the bottom.
If this tickles you the wrong way,
You are what is wrong with our western world.

16. Companion (Sonnet 1341 - 1343)

Sonnet 1341

The day you stop glorifying savages
like Churchill, Kissinger and Columbus,
I shall stop using Hitler as evidence
of your barbaric double standards.

It bothers me greatly to waste precious
pages mentioning names of animals.
I make it a point to not mention names,
unless absolutely essential.

We cannot lift up society
by dragging everyone down.
Focus on treating inhumanity,
not on fighting every idiot clown.

Sometimes the person is indeed the problem,
Then by all means fight till they lose all power.
But everyone you disagree with is not worth fighting,
Be very cautious not to let your rage take over.

Sonnet 1342

Rage is a rather potent force,
Don't waste it on idiots.
Reserve your rage for emergency,
Don't be slave to impulsiveness.

All that is old is not gold,
All that is new is not bold.
New or old, it's all the same,
When run by impulses same old.

Your impulse is just as mindless,
as those of your ancestors.
Our ancestors mistook impulse as enlightenment,
It's time we write new conscience parameters.

Benevolence is Bible supreme,
Conscience is living Koran.
Demolishing all donkey's dogma,
Being breaks free as Brahmakoran.

Note: To me everyone is equal, until they feel the urge to offer advise based on some stroneage tradition. That moment, I stop considering them as equal humans, and start treating them as adolescent children. Whenever you feel the audacity to advise a reformer, ask yourself this - what exactly have you done for the society that makes you qualified to judge a reformer? I sacrificed my youth for the world. What have you done? I put off starting a family for the world. What have you done? I obliterated my national and cultural identity for the world. What have you done? Till you've abolished the last trace of active bigotry, intolerance and fanatical fantasies from your mind, don't you dare touch my work. Everybody can quote Naskar, not everybody can accompany Naskar.

Sonnet 1343

Everyone is equal,
till they offer advise,
based not on conscience,
but on comforting lies.

Such people are no adult,
They must be cared as children.
Treat them like your offspring,
Who are in need of some lesson.

I sacrificed my youth for the world,
I put off starting family for the world.
If you have sacrificed more for society,
I'll obey your command word for word.

Till you've renounced all fanatical fantasies,
Don't you touch my work with your filthy hands!
Any ape can quote Naskar to suit their agenda,
Only humans can be Naskar's traveling companion.

17. Unvision (Sonnet 1344 - 1346)

Sonnet 1344

If you want, come and walk
beside me, not behind me.
If you cannot be light to yourself,
you're of no use to humanity.

World's light comes from your light,
It comes from the sacrifice of the few.
If these few ever became selfish,
Whole world would drown in dwindling dew.

Bodily birth is of no consequence,
If the mind is chained to the past.
If the mind never dawns with new light,
All synthetic light is useless dust.

Without the light of the individual heart,
Washington, Rome, all lose their glow.
Without the sight of a sentient civilian,
Apple vision is just unvision pro.

Paralyzed Reality
(The Sonnet, 1345)

Newspaper to smartphone,
rabbit r1 to apple vision pro,
social disconnection only
changes face, nothing more.

Nobody is busy enough
to need VR while walking.
People are meant to own tech,
Yet the opposite is happening.

Every tech has its place and purpose,
How many reminders are enough reminder!
First you buried your head in your phone,
Now you walk around as donkeys with blinker.

Companies are not to blame,
Real culprit is consumer idiocy.
In a world of unawareness,
VR and AR make paralyzed reality.

Sonnet 1346

Till you're aware of the reality of the world,
Augmented reality is but reality degraded.
Companies may peddle products for utopia,
State of the world is far from perfect.

No world is handed perfect,
World is perfected by hand.
We can't do that by escaping,
into a make believe virtual land.

It's okay to take momentary breaks, but
sooner or later you must come down to earth.
Cyberspace disconnected from societyspace,
is the making of a new kind of jungle world.

It's necessary to block out the noise sometimes,
But to do so permanently is an act of the ape.
To live in the world without bearing its burden,
is no advancement, but the mark of a savage.

18. Consensus (Sonnet 1347 - 1349)

Don't Have to Agree, to Love
(Sonnet 1347)

You don't have to agree with a person
completely, to love them - accept them.
There are a few, I disagree with plenty,
  yet till death, I'll fight for them.

Not all that Rumi wrote apply today,
yet I love Mevlana like my own brother.
Even more of Aquinas are out of date,
  yet like a friend I love my Thomas.

Heart doesn't care about consensus of the brain,
  Heart only cares for an inexplicable closeness.
Intellect has no bearing over heart's closeness,
  Often intellect is a barrier to life's wholeness.

Intellect is boon, but only when it helps wholeness.
Being right is not necessarily the mark of goodness.

What is Naskar
(The Sonnet, 1348)

Naskar is a culture unto themselves,
Naskar is a nation unto themselves.
Naskar is a planet unto themselves,
Naskar is a paradigm unto themselves.

Naskar culture is integration,
Naskar nation is world nation.
Naskar planet is borderless,
Naskar paradigm is undivision.

Naskar is not a he or she,
Naskar is the whole of humanity.
Naskar is neither east nor west,
Naskarosphere is conscious unity.

Naskar is just a lesser synonym,
The original name is Human Being.

Martyr's Dilemma
(An Existential Sonnet, 1349)

Abhijit Naskar are two, not one.
Abhijit the person, Naskar the mission.
Abhijit has dreams like an ordinary man,
While Naskar is the dream of world union.

Abhijit put his hopes and dreams away,
So that Naskar could engulf the world.
Abhijit even got dumped by the girl,
Because Naskar couldn't dump the world.

The question is, do I regret all this!
With all honesty - yes, I do on occasion.
All the vastness of Naskar isn't enough,
to make up for the things I missed out on.

The point is, it's okay to have regrets,
You ain't alive till you have regrets.
Yet I never abandoned my duty to the world,
For my mission is bigger than my regrets.

19. Mission (Sonnet 1350 - 1352)

Sonnet 1350

If you have no regrets, it means,
your mission isn't big enough.
Bigger the mission, more the regrets,
Regrets only strengthen our conviction.

Everybody wants to change the world,
that's no biggie - the real question is,
can you spend your whole life working
for the world, without any recognition!

If you can, then you are a humanitarian.
If you can, then you are a reformer.
If you can, then you are a peacemaker,
If you can, then you are a world builder.

Unleash your dreams past regrets 'n recognition.
You are the world's gateway to invigoration.

Sonnet 1351

Mission is the vision,
Mission is invigoration.
Mind and mission as one spirit,
lay the labor of illumination.

True mission doesn't suppress regrets,
True mission simply overwhelms regrets.
True mission isn't without expectation,
True mission simply works regardless.

Life of mission is a love affair,
an affair with vision unfading,
a vision that makes you almost blind,
to all selfish pleasures of living.

My mission is my happiness,
so the world can have a serene life.
In love, the greatest pleasure
is the pleasure of sacrifice.

Vulnerable Love
(The Sonnet, 1352)

Choose me if you feel something,
not because it's convenient or glorious.
I have neither the interest nor the strength,
to go out again and look for someone else.

If you choose me, you are stuck with me,
through thick and thin, through everything.
It won't always be clear and sunny,
sometimes it'll be blue, sometimes boring.

True love is not something you find,
True love is something you nurture together.
Once you rediscover yourself in someone,
Never turn your back, come hell or high water!

Any ape can find escape in romance novels,
It takes a human to be the living pillar of love.
While every robot seeks emotional maturity,
Be the human who cherishes vulnerable love.

Note: In love there is no controlling each other.
Because, in love there is no each, there is no other, it's
all one organic existence, ever vigilant of combined
nourishment - ever responsible for combined growth

- ever aware of combined welfare. Desire for control is born of separation - where there is no separation, there is no need for control. And the same applies to geopolitics.

When nations are separated, all they want is one thing - to control each other. But when there is no separation amongst nations, there is no tendency of control - and where there is no control, there is no war. And to this, every freaking bureaucrat, politician and diplomat will mock me as a romanticist. To which I can only say - if a world without weapons of mass destruction sounds like impractical romanticism to you, then I'm afraid, you have not come far from your savage days in the jungle, my dear apes!

Before being sworn into office, every head of state should spend a week in space, gathering some sense of the insurmountable gravity of our little blue home in the unfathomable vastness of the cosmos. Perhaps then when they return to earth, they could actually work for the benefit of the people of earth, rather than wasting their term in office like yet another tribal savage obsessing over petty nationalistic agenda.

20. Untethered (Sonnet 1353 - 1355)

How to Train Your Head of State
(The Sonnet, 1353)

We shall achieve more by
blasting politicians into space,
than by blasting satellites
to other planets.

They'll leave earth as warmongers,
and return as peacemakers.
They'll leave earth as mindless apes,
and return as mindful humans.

In the middle of absolute vacuum,
mind grows fond of the warmth of home.
Fondness born of existential crisis,
never subsides even after you return
to your comfort zone.

When you are floating in space untethered,
each speck of earthland is equally priceless.
Then you'll realize the fallacy of borders -
Nation-nonsense will fade,
and earth will be your primary sense.

Humanitarian Arithmetic
(Sonnet 1354)

If it takes $300bn to end world hunger,
and 7 trillion to fund the next AI wonder,
how many people have to starve to death,
to feed the appetite of the cyberworld?

If Britain's NHS costs about $200bn,
and US military costs 800 billion dollars,
how many have to suffer from sickness,
for the tribal chiefs to feel secure?

If it takes $20bn to end homelessness
in the US, and trillions to colonize Mars,
how many have to sleep in cardboard boxes,
for heirs of billionaires to breed on Mars?

You don't need to be a Ramanujan or Euler,
to solve this simple arithmetic equation.
But you do need a living human heart,
to take responsibility for the solution.

Sonnet 1355

What I have written in ten years,
will last for over 10,000 years.
In the process, one man's nonduality
will flood the world with humanitarians.

One man's restless nights
will flood the world with heralds of dawn.
One man's call for unification
will fire up the veins with divine brawn.

My divinity comes from my heart,
My brawn comes from my backbone.
Add to that a curious brain,
You are an army of your own.

I've spent my life leaving behind
an inexhaustible supply of electricity,
which won't let the hearts dampen,
till everywhere there is love and liberty.

Note: Much of my work may go over your head, that's alright - return after a few years. Barring my first ten or so straightforward works, different parts of my vast interdisciplinary oeuvre would make sense at different stages of mental development, both of the individual and the species. Therefore, if something doesn't make sense to you at the moment, don't rush - live your life, and return after some years. But mark you, still many things might not make sense even when you are old and frail - it doesn't mean you have failed me, it means you've done your bit to realize me, now it's time for the next generation to pick up where you've left off. If you figure out everything there is to know about the sun, there'll be nothing left for the future generations to explore. And remember, I am just the portal, cosmos is the writer.

21. Rooted (Sonnet 1356 - 1358)

Sonnet 1356

I am just the portal,
Cosmos is the writer.
There's nothing supernatural,
I am just a cosmic mirror.

We are but nature's reflection,
In our hands unfolds world's destiny.
We are the pages, we are the ink.
I am the world, the world is me.

Thus speaks the human divine,
whose divinity is rooted in life.
All other divinity are ancient fakes,
there's no other light but life.

When you are alive,
whole cosmos comes to life.
Blind faith is not divinity,
It's a desecration of life.

Sonnet 1357

We don't need to cook up supernatural fantasies
to be aware of the pricelessness of life.
In fact, the supernatural often undermines life,
by disconnecting us from our innate light.

Focus on life, focus on culture,
not just your own, but of another.
Anybody can boast of things their own,
It takes character to be one with another.

Language is magic, culture is magic,
I wield that magic in my breath.
My brain is a symphony of portals,
Each transcending past exclusivity,
into distinct linguocultural awareness.

Learn a skill, earn a living.
Learn a language, earn a life.
Adopt etiquette, attract shallow respect.
Adopt a culture, attract love and light.

Sonnet 1358

Kids often ask me innocently,
Do I believe in ghosts and goblins!
Remember this, and remember it well:
There is no greater God than you,
there is no spookier ghost than you.

God complex is a useful faculty,
If it eliminates inferiority complex.
Know your strengths and nourish 'em well,
Never let nothing dominate your valiance!

Idiots would take this
as passport to smugness.
True Gods would know,
Godliness means responsibleness.

Be God and behave as God,
Take the world on your shoulders.
If the heart doesn't bleed for others,
Prayers and meditation are worthless.

22. Intention (Sonnet 1359 - 1361)

Sonnet 1359

I know people who use God
as excuse for hate and war.
I know people who use God
as inspiration for love and peace.

I know people who use Science
as excuse to be cold and inhuman.
I know people who use Science
as means to be warm and responsible.

It's neither God nor Science,
that causes coldness and war.
In the hands of a selfish ape,
Science and God are equally impotent.

But when it's a responsible human
that wields either God or Science,
You can rest assured of one thing,
nothing can dent their humanness.

Only Bow to Love
(Sonnet 1360)

I don't bow to truth,
Truth is my toy.
I don't bow to science,
Science is my toy.
I don't bow to law,
Law is my slave.
I don't bow to wealth,
All wealth end in ashes.
I don't bow to no constitution,
I pen constitutions in my sleep.
No holy writ is my authority,
I pour out holiness on a daily basis.
I am love, I only bow to love.
Till I sleep, everyday I fall anew.
Facts, faith, law, go get in line.
When I see fit, I'll call you.

Note: This is my note to the scientists - a repeated note that is. We do science, not for the sake of science, but for the sake of humanity. If you remove human welfare from the equation, all you are left with is a fancy toy.

Sonnet 1361

What all these have to do with
demilitarization, one wonders!
That's indeed a valid question.
We cannot demilitarize the world,
without detribalizing the citizens.

And we cannot detribalize the citizens,
without pouring love into the world.
We cannot pour love into the world,
without being love incarnate ourselves.

I am not talking about some petty lust,
masquerading as fancy cinematic love.
I'm talking about total annihilation of self,
in absolute unification of the universe.

Militariless world starts with tribeless minds,
For all war is born of tribal minds.
Borders in mind produce borders in world,
Peace on earth comes from borderless minds.

23. Concern (Sonnet 1362 - 1364)

Sonnet 1362

Borders in mind produce borders in world,
Divided minds produce all shallow woe.
Sin is in eyes, not in dress.
Evil lies in intention, not in clothes.

Cleanse your mind of all filth,
Only then the world will rise pious.
Piety doesn't mean mythical magicality,
True piousness is the magic of kindness.

When the heart contains the world,
That's the sign of a divine heart.
Yet you keep chasing myths 'n fantasies,
overlooking the obvious miracle of heart!

Mindfulness leads to selflessness, which
unfolds as mindlessness is left behind.
Peace begins when the mind is whole,
when mind is kind to another mind.

Mission over Recognition
(The Sonnet, 1363)

Let me show you what is
action without expectation!
What is it to do your duty,
without regard for recognition!

Quite often I lose count of my works,
Yet I've never had a fancy book launch.
I write in silence, I release in silence,
I have no relation to praise and applause.

I am the peak of humanitarian literature,
All without an ounce of support or award.
I am not a writer, I am world reformer,
My first concern is an integrated world.

Whatever happens next, know that it had
nothing to do with the making of a mission.
It's easy to bask in the glory of the sun,
not so much to fuel solar combustion.

Sonnet 1364

Take not the ridicule seriously,
Take not the applause seriously.
Take only your mission seriously,
Don't ever slacken out of tenacity.

Applause has a way of rendering us lazy,
Ridicule has a way of making us bitter.
Enduring both if you can stay on track,
Then you are the rightful dreamworker.

Timing for a dream is never right,
Yet you must persevere against the tide.
A tenacious mind can turn any table,
Even amidst the utter absence of light.

If one sun can illuminate nine planets,
One mind can definitely illuminate one.
But if you give in to every clap-n-scorn,
You are no explorer of illumination.

24. Mirror (Sonnet 1365 - 1367)

Celestial Passenger
(The Sonnet, 1365)

Producing a celestial humanitarian legacy,
I don't care for praise and applause.
Now I just want to leave behind something
personal for every culture in the world.

That's why I started to rewrite some sonnets,
in languages I've grown fond of over the years.
I know I can't possibly cover every culture,
But rest assured, I'll embolden much of the tears.

I am the world I want to build,
I am the human I want to inspire.
I am the mind I want as neighbor,
I am just a glimpse into the future.

Assimilate all, alienate none.
Be the unbent explorer of illumination.
Be the pilgrim of living piety,
Celestial passenger you, go find a mirror!

Sonnet 1366

Without people, I am a dead scientist.
With people, I am a living scientist.
Without people, I am a dead humanist.
With people, I am a living humanist.
Without people, I am a dead theologian.
With people, I am a living theologian.
Without people, I am a dead humanitarian.
With people, I am a living humanitarian.
Without people, I am a dead philosopher.
With people, I am a living philosopher.
Without people, I am poetic fiction.
With people, I am living poetic wonder.
It's people that bring theories to life.
Disconnected from people, all books are lie.
People are the line between life and death.
If you are with people, then you are alive.

Sonnet 1367

In an ailing world of theories,
Be the living cure of practice.
In a world teeming with wannabe rulers,
Be the self-appointed insignia of service.

Chase the sea, not the shore,
The shore is for cowardly apes.
Use the shore for occasional resets,
not as your permanent residence.

Now let's transcend both shore and sea,
Then you shall clearly see.
There's a sea in every shore,
There's a shore in every sea.

Shore and sea are states of mentality.
There's no distance between shore and sea.

25. Attention (Sonnet 1368 - 1370)

Sonnet 1368

Before all shore and sea,
Find yourself an anchor.
Life is strong when anchor is strong,
Person or mission, to which you're tethered.

Difference between tether
and chain is in intention,
the later cripples life's motion,
while the former empowers ascension.

True tether is never an obstacle,
It's no tether, if it causes obstruction.
The mightiest device needs a grounding wire,
The mightiest heart needs a homing beacon.

You're the beacon to the world,
But you too need a beacon.
I can't tell what or who that is,
Beacon is what helps you stay human.

Sonnet 1369

In the early days I used to have a podcast,
which was kinda supplement to my books.
But once my magic was fully awakened,
I abandoned it after a few books.

I had to abandon all distractions,
So I could put all attention on writing.
There is no room for distractions,
If your mission is world building.

Choose one thing and give it your all,
Abandon any activity that is extra.
Not talking about occasional leisure,
But any task that draws brain power,
yet doesn't replenish your heart.

I don't have any leisure activity as such,
Writing is my leisure, it's my way of being.
But you may need some kind of leisure act,
Resort to it for charge, but never stop working.

Miracle and Migraine
(Sonnet 1370)

Words are my leisure,
Words are my life.
Words are my gift to thee,
Use 'em wisely for light.

Kind words cost us nothing,
Cruel words will cost us all.
Faith in people costs us nothing,
Systemic mistrust will end us all.

It is common knowledge in the circle,
I don't control words, I get visions.
However, every miracle takes its toll,
Hence, the migraines are getting worse.

I don't mind, so long as I am ointment.
You keep the magic, I'll keep the pain.

Note: There is nothing supernatural about visions - or to be more accurate, contrary to traditional belief, it's not messages from some extraterrestrial domain. Visions are indeed messages from a mysterious realm alright, but like the everyday realm of human perception, the transcendental realm as well is creation of brain chemicals. I won't go into details here, as I already did that in my early days. One of my earliest works, Autobiography of God, contains a detailed analytical account of the neurobiology of transcendental experiences. However, the question is not whether there is an explanation, the question is, is it worth explaining! Because, while sometimes the lack of explanation facilitates superstition, some things are better left unexplained - such as, love.

26. Guts (Sonnet 1371 - 1373)

Sonnet 1371

Contrary to traditional belief,
Visions are nothing supernatural.
They are not messages from heaven,
But from the domain neurological.

Like the everyday realm of perception,
Transcendental realm is born of chemicals.
All our experiences, normal, paranormal,
Are natural generation of neurochemicals.

I won't go into the details here,
for I did that in my early days.
My earliest works include definitive texts,
on the neurology of mystical experiences.

Question is not whether there is an explanation,
Question is, do you want an explanation!
Some experiences are better left unexplained,
Sometimes unexplanation aids superstition.

Sonnet 1372

No pain, no ointment.
No curse, no miracle.
Every blessing has its burden,
Someone's gotta be responsible.

You can sit and sob over
your wounds all you want,
That won't heal the wounds,
nor will it make you strong.

Let the wounds sink in character,
Overwhelm them with a vision,
Wounds embraced is the beginning
of strength and illumination.

No Himalaya rises on smooth grounds,
Only through existential upheaval
does the Everest soar past clouds.

Sonnet 1373

Have you got no guts, o human,
To live as a human being!
Have you got no brain, o human,
To defy all prejudice scheme!

Have you got no backbone, human,
To stand unbent with dignity!
Have you got no heart, o human,
To bleed in pain for humanity!

Have you got no conscience, human,
To tell the right from wrong!
Have you got no blood, o human,
To boil for justice and burn!

Truth is not the journey
from one veil to another.
Truth involves peeling the veil
one layer after another.
Will you now stand human, o human!
Justice begins with you, not another.

27. Transcend (Sonnet 1374 - 1376)

Sonnet 1374

Truth is not an expedition
from one veil to another.
Truth involves peeling the veil
one layer after another.

Love is not a jungle safari
from one hunt to another.
Love is a sacred calling
of losing oneself in another.

Only with such love
we shall revive the world.
Only with such truth
we shall reform the world.

Peace begins with truth,
Truth begins with love.
Peace is no job for law,
Peace begins when with the world
civilians fall in love.

Sonnet 1375

World needs love that transcends body.
World needs truth that transcends belief.
World needs honor that transcends wealth.
World needs order that transcends police.

You're the bridge between world and humanity.
You're the wall between world and humanity.
Break yourself against your practical judgment,
So you're reborn in love, as you're meant to be.

The world is swarming with snakes,
In your soul brews the antidote.
Churn your doubts, burn your dread,
One gentle gaze sanitizes the cosmos.

In this world desensitized by coldness
and hypnotized by cruelty,
be the sanity that sanitizes society,
out of the swamp of stereotype cacophony.

Note: They ask me, why aren't you still properly known in the mainstream! Well, the Himalayas have been standing for 40 million years, yet it's only in the last century that humans first climbed Everest. They are oblivious of me, because once you get addicted to

the transcendental terrains of the Himalayas, all your
superficial little molehills will crumble to dust.

Sonnet 1376

Why am I still not mainstream popular,
They often ask me in an act of mockery!
Well, Himalaya's been standing for 40mn yrs,
Yet humans didn't climb till last century.

It's easier to be hypnotized by flashlights,
than embark into the vastness of the sun.
Once you get addicted to Himalayan terrains,
superficial little molehills crumble to dust.

They are oblivious of me, because I ain't
entertaining, nor do I chase publicity.
One page of my work holds ample thunder,
to destroy all self-centric sanity.

It doesn't matter to the Everest whether
eight people climb it or eight billion.
The sun doesn't care whether one planet benefits
or nine, the sun only burns for illumination.

28. Make Life (Sonnet 1377 - 1379)

Sonnet 1377

If you want to burn,
burn not to make an impression,
Burn so you could bring light,
Burn so you trigger invigoration.

If you want to smile,
smile not with an agenda,
Smile without hidden deceit,
Smile just as a vessel of cheer.

If you want to serve,
serve not to take selfies,
Serve to lift up yourself,
Serve to end human miseries.

If you want to burn,
burn for the sake of light.
Burn beyond all learned night,
Burn to end all human fright.

Sonnet 1378

Books and literature are not the same thing,
you can have a shelf stacked with books
yet not an ounce of literature.

Facts and science are not the same thing,
you can memorize all the facts in the world,
yet not have an ounce of scientific understanding.

Scripture and divinity are not the same thing,
you can memorize all the hymns and ayats,
yet spend your existence as a divine vacuum.

Intellect and wisdom are not the same thing,
Google is the most intellectual entity on earth,
yet a ten year old human is wiser than google.

Books and literature are not the same thing,
Books mean sales, literature means substance.
Survival and existence are not the same thing,
Survival is avoiding death, to make life is existence.

Sonnet 1379

Survival means avoiding death,
Existence means making a life.
Knowledge means reading books,
Wisdom means realizing light.

Knowledge doesn't make you a good human,
Unless you are aware of life's fragility.
Being smart and being human are not the same,
Neither computer nor animal makes human company.

True literature brings you closer to the soil,
True wisdom makes you humble and selfless.
If you turn cold and mechanical instead,
You are not learned, you are just dead.

Survival means avoiding death,
Existence means making a life.
Any animal can avoid death,
It takes a human to make a life.

29. Backyard (Sonnet 1380 - 1382)

Sonnet 1380

Any animal can avoid death,
It takes a human to truly live.
Any animal can wage war,
It takes a human to make peace.

Any animal can attend peace talks,
with nuclear weapons in their backyard.
It takes a human to rise above weapons,
and actually take a stand peacewards.

Talking of peace is ridiculously easy,
Doing what it takes takes character.
Any monkey can defend their tribe,
Takes a human to be world's caretaker.

I have one question for humankind.
If you are so advanced and civilized,
why are you yet to ban weapons of all kind?

Sonnet 1381

How come we can fit the world
in our pocket, but not in our heart!
We can transmit messages across the world,
yet can't hear the teardrops of our neighbor!

How come we can send rockets to other planets,
yet we can't take care of our own planet!
How come governments can fund war after war,
yet can't feed and shelter the homeless!

All the wars in the world are government-funded,
Try to get your head around this simple truth.
If you still cannot see the irony of the matter,
You better head back to your jungle roots.

While buying groceries you bargain like crazy,
Yet you never think twice, funding stately paranoia.
Citizens fund the war, citizens pay the price,
While politicians party under diplomatic umbrella.

Sonnet 1382

Greed comes from a rotten core,
Nourish the core 'n there is peace.
Love is an act of courage,
Hate is an act of cowardice.

Throw all fear in the trash,
Most of them ain't yours to begin with.
Prejudice is just the symptom,
of a mind existentially constipated.

Let neither politicians nor ancestors
contaminate your senses with fear.
Modern sapiens must be modern enough to
not succumb to the army of ancient monsters.

Love is an act of bravery,
Hate is an act of fear.
Pilgrim of piety are you,
Prejudice is not your savior.

30. Lie Awake (Sonnet 1383 - 1385)

Ancestry is Garbage
(The Sonnet, 1383)

DNA test may reveal your ancestry,
But there is no DNA test for character.
IQ may reveal deficit in logical aptitude,
There's no IQ test for excellence or genius.

If bloodline dictated destiny,
We'd still be dangling from trees.
Not that we've done much better,
But at least there is possibility.

In the end we are all monkeys,
We all come from the jungle.
Question is, have we conquered
the jungle that lurks in our heart,
have we risen yet above the animal!

Ancestry is garbage, IQ is useless,
Living humans don't rely on such nonsense.
Heart, brain, backbone, these make who we are,
Everything else is mythology of the savages.

Sonnet 1384

Enough with back to the future,
Enough with back to the past!
Open your eyes, come back to present.

Enough with worship of golden chains,
Enough with worship of silicon chips!
Open your eyes to life's luminescence.

If you cared about the singularity of mind and mind,
as much as the singularity of mind and machine,
the world would've been at a much better place.

If you cared about easing the suffering of the living,
than pleasing the fanatic fantasies of dead relics,
the world would've been at a much better place.

Enough with back to the future,
Enough with back to the past!
Open your eyes to the present,
and wake up as lovers.

Sonnet 1385

Science fiction has its place,
Study of history has its place.
But nothing must undermine life now,
It's all supposed to elevate the present.

Elevation of the present doesn't mean,
External elevation of selective community.
Elevation of the present actually means,
Complete elevation of humanity, mind and body.

Till you lie awake in bed thinking
of the world, you ain't awake at all.
Till you lie awake in bed worrying
for the helpless, you ain't alive at all.

There is no magical secret to sustainability.
We are the secret we seek in myths and technology.

31. Outlaw (Sonnet 1386 - 1388)

Sonnet 1386

You are the secret you seek to find,
You are the magic most divine.
You are the light of its own kind,
Your place is in the field,
not in the sidelines.

You can't build society from the sidelines,
You can't initiate peace from the sidelines.
You can't do nothing from the sidelines,
Human you are, to humans be the lifeline!

You are the miracle you seek in church,
You are the gospel you seek in bible.
You are the reason behind civilization,
You are the mutation out of the jungle.

You are the truth you seek in myths.
You are the cure to mindless malice.

Sonnet 1387

You are the curse,
You are the cure.
You are the ocean,
You are the oar.

Mind finite is Human,
Mind infinite is God.
Mind bound is leech,
Mind unbound is Lord.

Mind exclusive is savage,
Mind inclusive is civilized.
Mind contracting is dead,
Mind expanding is alive.

Mind bound is animal,
Mind unbound is divine.
Mind divided means world divided,
Mind united leads to humankind.

Sonnet 1388

Divide and divine can never go together,
If they do, you are worshiping a lie.
Greed and science can never go together,
If they do, you are but a scientific lie.

Human potential must make way for oneness,
If it doesn't, it is but potential wasted.
All brain power must be used with collectivity,
If it is not, it's brain power desecrated.

If science doesn't make you selfless,
You are studying the wrong kind of science.
If faith doesn't make you one with others,
You are practicing but a primitive faith.

Oneness, inclusion, nonduality,
it's all one divine law.
Where there is no oneness,
all light is outlaw.

32. Divine (Sonnet 1389 - 1391)

Sonnet 1389

Yesterday's divinity cannot be today's divinity,
Yesterday's science cannot be today's science.
Both must be rooted in concern for collective life,
Without which, science, faith, both require defiance.

What does this have to do with peace,
What does this have to do with demilitarization!
If that's what you are really wondering,
You've understood nothing from the beginning to end.

Peace, divine, science, it's all one existential spirit,
They are all intrinsically entangled with one another.
In fact, there is no another, for it's all one,
One spectacular force manifesting in diverse manner.

Divinity is my science, my science is divine.
But alas, you can't fathom it with mere intellect!
You gotta surpass both intellect and obedience,
Only then your heart will lead to a peaceful place.

Sonnet 1390

Discard all trace of obedience,
both to logic and tradition.
Only then the human shall emerge,
out of the confines of prison.

Logic without heart is prison,
Faith without heart is prison.
Everything without heart is prison,
Takes a human to foster realization.

Then there is the prison of politics,
Where every prisoner feels like the boss.
So they drag the society down with them,
And not a single civilian utters a word!

For the world to change, civilians must change.
Not constitution, not holy books, but human heart
is the source of all civilization and sentience.

Sonnet 1391

You can't make peace,
till you are divine.
You can't be divine,
till you come to life.

You can't do science,
till you are responsible.
You can't be responsible,
till you are one with all.

Progress, divinity, all will come,
First you gotta stand as human being.
Daring tech and daring text are
equally worthless, if wielded by a fancy fiend.

You can't make peace,
till you are divine.
There is no greater divinity,
than the love for humankind.

33. Glue (Sonnet 1392 - 1394)

Sonnet 1392

Religion without oneness is lame,
Science without accountability is shame.
Philosophy without gentleness is vain,
Vision without virtue is inane.

Religion begins with realization,
Science begins with realization,
Philosophy begins with realization,
Without realization there's only degradation.

Curiosity is the lifeblood of science,
not constant boasting of lifeless facts.
Realization is the birth of divinity,
not the memorizing of ancient books.

Till we make the world our divine dome,
We shall know no tranquility realm.
Till humankind is our home,
We shall know no home.

Sonnet 1393

You are the God,
You are the rock.
You are the tune
on the cosmic chord.

You are the good,
You are the news.
You are the good news
of motion upward.

You are the sum of all science,
You are the life of all poetry.
You are the end to animosity,
You are the answer to conspiracy.

You are the peace to a peaceless world.
You are the glue that joins all upward.

Sonnet 1394

You are the glue
to this worldly crew.
You are the torch
when the clouds brew.

You are the intelligence,
You are the design,
There is no other force,
To forge the world anew.

You are the world's destiny,
The world is your design.
You are not godless,
You are godliness alive.

Real education is
to learn what to unlearn.
You are the world,
the world is your mission.

34. Travel (Sonnet 1395 - 1397)

Sonnet 1395

The bridge is you,
The seed is you,
The divine answer
to chaos is you.

The kite is you,
The knight is you.
Sail across the clouds,
Riding your wounds anew.

I know you are tired,
But march on anyway.
Be sight to the sightless,
Pen with pain to chart the way.

You are the breeze,
you are the brave.
You are the motion
of time and space.

Sonnet 1396

Love is a travel
from chaff to core.
Love is to dismantle
all dividing abhor.

Love is the thread
that sutures society.
Love is the ointment
that engulfs duality.

Love is not christian,
Love is not muslim.
Names are mere reflection,
Love is the source beam.

Love is lament,
Love is torment.
Walk past the self,
And love is ascent.

Sonnet 1397

Love is travel,
Love is reform.
Peace is play,
When love reigns dawn.

If politicians disappear from
the world, world will flourish.
If lovers disappear from
the world, world will wither.

Forget policy, just love the world,
Love the world like your first love.
When each nation has such crazy lovers,
There'll be no need for fancy peace talks.

Love is travel, love is reform.
Peace will come on its own,
When lovers hail the dawn.

35. Present (Sonnet 1398 – 1400)

Sonnet 1398

Without you there is no peace,
Without you there is no love.
You are the source 'n sink of it all,
Without you there is no civilized world.

Wake up, my friend!
Wake up from wakefulness.
Wakefulness that pampers ego,
is wakefulness of the leeches.

Wake up, o hero!
Wake up civil, wake up divine!
To hell with fancy constitutions!
You are the key to all illusive strife.

Constitution that peddles military,
belongs in the trash.
Scripture that peddles hate,
belongs in the trash.

Laws written by dead people don't apply
to the living, if you don't get that,
you are already dead.

Sonnet 1399

Problem is neither constitution,
nor scripture, real problem is rigidity.
When you can't tell right from wrong,
on your own, you're the root of insanity.

More than the world, be aware of yourself,
Self conquered is world conquered.
You are the problem, you are the path,
Self conquered is hate conquered.

Path unfolds when person unfolds,
Peace unfolds when mind expands.
World unites when martyr ignites,
Present prospers when person stands.

Person is the peace,
person is the present.
Person is hindrance,
person is the help.

Sonnet 1400

Person is the present,
Person is the gift.
Person is the stairs,
Person is the lift.

Person is the help,
Person is the hand.
Person is the feet,
on which time stands.

Person is the shoulder,
Person is the head.
Person is the mission,
Person is the message.

Let tears flow when it's cloudy,
Stand unarmed while arrows fly.
In a nuclear world of talks and deceit,
Militaristic peace is a democratic lie.

BIBLIOGRAPHY

Archer M., (2000), Being Human: The Problem of Agency. Cambridge University Press.

Adolphs R (2003) Cognitive neuroscience of human social behaviour. Nature Rev Neurosci 4: 165–178.

Adolphs R, Tranel D, Damasio AR (2003) Dissociable neural systems for recognizing emotions. Brain Cogn 52: 61–69.

Andresen, Jensine, and Robert Forman, eds. Cognitive Models and Spiritual Maps. Bowling Green, Ohio: Imprint Academic, 2000.

Azari, Nina, Janpeter Nickel, Gilbert Wunderlich, Michael Niedeggen, Harald Hefter, Lutz Tellmann, Hans Herzog, Petra Stoerig, Dieter Birnbacher, and Rudiger Seitz. "Neural

Correlates of Religious Experience." European Journal of Neuroscience 13, no. 8 (2001)

Agar, N. (2004). Liberal eugenics: In defence of human enhancement. London: Blackwell Publishing.

Bernstein R.J., (1976), The Restructuring Social and Political Thought.

Bernstein R.J., (1983), Beyond Relativism and Objectivism: Science, Hermeneutics, and Praxis. Philadelphia: University of Pennsylvania Press.

Bernstein R.J., (1986), Philosophical Profiles. Philadelphia: University of Pennsylvania Press.

Birkhead, T. R., Johnson, S. D. & Nettleship, D. N. (1985). Extra-pair matings and mate guarding in the common murre Uria aalge. - Anim. Behav. 33, p. 608-619.

Beauregard, Mario, and Vincent Paquette. "Neural Correlates of a Mystical Experience in Carmelite Nuns." Neuroscience Letters 405, no. 3 (2006)

Benson, Herbert. Timeless Healing: The Power and Biology of Belief. New York: Scribner, 1996

Bose, Subhas Chandra. An Indian Pilgrim: An Unfinished Autobiography, Oxford University Press, 1997

Bogen, J.E.(1995a), 'On the neurophysiology of consciousness: Part I. An overview', Consciousness and Cognition, 4.

Bogen, J.E. (1995b), 'On the neurophysiology of consciousness: Part II. Constraining the semantic problem', Consciousness and Cognition, 4.

Bremner, J. D., R. Soufer, et al. (2001). "Gender differences in cognitive and neural correlates of remembrance of emotional words." Psychopharmacol Bull 35 (3).

Brothers, L. (2002). The social brain: A project for integrating primate behavior and neurophysiology in a new domain. In J. T. Cacioppo et al. (Eds.), Foundations in neuroscience. Cambridge, MA: MIT Press.

Buss, D. D. (2003). Evolutionary Psychology: The New Science of Mind, 2nd ed. New York: Allyn & Bacon.

Buss, D. M. (1989). "Conflict between the sexes: Strategic interference and the evocation of anger and upset." J Pers Soc Psychol 56 (5).

Buss, D. M. (1995). "Psychological sex differences. Origins through sexual selection." Am Psychol 50 (3).

Buss, D. M., and D. P. Schmitt (1993). "Sexual strategies theory: An evolutionary perspective on human mating." Psychol Rev 100 (2).

Blakemore SJ, Decety J (2001) From the perception of action to the understanding of intention. Nature Rev Neurosci 2: 561.

Carr L, Iacoboni M, Dubeau MC, Mazziotta JC, Lenzi GL (2003) Neural mechanisms of empathy in humans: a relay from neural systems for imitation to limbic areas. Proc Natl Acad Sci USA 100: 5497–5502.

Chomsky Noam, (2017) Requiem for the American Dream

Chomsky Noam, (2016) Who Rules the World?

Chomsky Noam, (2010) How the World Works

Churchland, P.S. (1986), Neurophilosophy (Cambridge, MA: The MIT Press).

Churchland, P.S. & Ramachandran, V.S. (1993), 'Filling in: Why Dennett is wrong', in Dennett and His Critics:

Demystifying Mind, ed. B. Dahlbom (Oxford: Blackwell Scientific Press).

Churchland, P.S., Ramachandran, V.S. & Sejnowski, T.J. (1994), 'A critique of pure vision', in Large- scale Neuronal Theories of the Brain, ed. C. Koch & J.L. Davis (Cambridge, MA: The MIT Press).

Coyle EF. Integration of the physiological factors determining endurance performance ability. Exerc Sport Sci Rev. 1995;23:25–63.

Crick, F. (1994), The Astonishing Hypothesis: The Scientific Search for the Soul (New York: Simon and Schuster).

Crick, F. (1996), 'Visual perception: rivalry and consciousness', Nature, 379.

Crick, F. & Koch, C. (1992), 'The problem of consciousness', Scientific American, 267.

Damasio, A (2003a) Looking for Spinoza. Harcourt Inc. Damasio A (2003b) Feeling of emotion and the self. Ann NY Acad Sci 1001: 253–261.

d'Aquili, Eugene. "Senses of Reality in Science and Religion." Zygon 17, no 4 (1982)

d'Aquili, Eugene. "The Biopsychological Determinants of Religious Ritual Behavior." Zygon 10, no. 1 (1975)

Daly DD. 1958. Ictal affect. Am J Psychiatry.

Damasio, A. (1999) The Feeling of What Happens: Body, Emotion and the Making of Consciousness. London, Heinemann.

Darwin, C. (1859) On the Origin of Species by Means of Natural Selection. London, Murray.

Darwin, C. (1871) The Descent of Man and Selection in Relation to Sex. London, John Murray.

Darwin, C. (1872) The Expression of the Emotions in Man and Animals. London, John Murray; also published 1965, Chicago, University of Chicago Press.

Dawkins, R. (1976) The Selfish Gene. Oxford, Oxford University Press; a new edition, with additional material, was published in 1989.

Dewhurst, Kenneth, and A. W. Beard. "Sudden Religious Conversions in Temporal Lobe Epilepsy." British Journal of Psychiatry 117 (1970)

Dewhurst K, Beard AW. Sudden religious conversions in temporal lobe epilepsy. 1970 Epilepsy Behav 2003

Devinsky O, Lai G. Spirituality and religion in epilepsy. Epilepsy Behav 2008.

Devinsky, O., Morrell, MJ, Vogt, BA. (1995) 'Contribution of anterior cingulate cortex to behavior', Brain, 118.

E. Horvitz, "One Hundred Year Study on Artificial Intelligence: Reflections and Framing," ed: Stanford University, 2014.

Eckhart Meister, Selected Writings

Farah, M.J. (1989), 'The neural basis of mental imagery', Trends in Neurosciences, 10.

Freud, S. "The Interpretation of Dreams", 1900

Freud, S. "Selected papers on hysteria and other psychoneuroses" Journal of Nervous and Mental Disease 1909.

Freud, S. "The Origin and Development of Psychoanalysis", 1910

Freud, S. "Psychopathology of everyday life", 1914

Freud, S. "Beyond the Pleasure Principle", 1920

Frith, C.D. & Dolan, R.J. (1997), 'Abnormal beliefs: Delusions and memory', Paper presented at the May, 1997, Harvard Conference on Memory and Belief.

Gray JA. The Psychology of Fear and Stress. 2nd ed. New York, NY: Cambridge University Press; 1988.

Gloor, P. (1992), 'Amygdala and temporal lobe epilepsy', in The Amygdala: Neurobiological Aspects of Emotion, Memory and Mental Dysfunction, ed J.P. Aggleton (New York: Wiley-Liss).

Grady, D. (1993), 'The vision thing: Mainly in the brain', Discover, June.

Gallese V, Keysers C, Rizzolatti G (2004) A unifying view of the basis of social cognition. Trends Cogn Sci 8: 396–403.

Guevara Che, The Motorcycle Diaries, 1992

Hari R, Forss N, Avikainen S, Kirveskari S, Salenius S, Rizzolatti G (1998) Activation of human primary motor cortex during action observation: a neuromagnetic study. Proc. Natl Acad Sci USA 95: 15061–15065.

Hardy, G. H. (1940). Ramanujan. Cambridge: Cambridge University Press.

Hall, Daniel, Keith Meador, and Harold Koenig. "Measuring Religiousness in Health Research: Review and Critique." Journal of Religion and Health 47, no. 2 (2008)

Harris, Sam, Jonas Kaplan, Ashley Curiel, Susan Bookheimer, Marco Iacoboni, and Mark Cohen. "The Neural Correlates of Religious and Nonreligious Belief." PLoS One 4, no. 10 (October 1, 2009)

Halgren, E. (1992), 'Emotional neurophysiology of the amygdala within the context of human cognition', in The Amygdala: Neurobiological Aspects of Emotion, Memory and Mental Dysfunction, ed J.P. Aggleton (New York: Wiley-Liss).

Handbook of Emotions, Edited by Michael Lewis, Jeannette M. Haviland-Jones, and Lisa Feldman Barrett, The Guilford Press; 3rd edition (2010).

Hameroff, S.R. and Penrose, R. (1996) Conscious events as orchestrated space-time selections. Journal of Consciousness Studies 3(1), 36-53; also reprinted in J. Shear (ed.) (1997) Explaining Consciousness-The Hard Problem. Cambridge, MA, MIT Press, 177-95.

Haugeland, J. (ed.) (1997) Mind Design II: Philosophy, Psychology, Artificial Intelligence. Cambridge, MA, MIT Press.

Hauser, M.D. (2000) Wild Minds: What Animals Really Think. New York, Henry Holt and Co.; London, Penguin.

Hebb, D.O. (1949) The Organization of Behavior. New York, Wiley.

Hess, EH (1975) "The role of pupil size in communication," Scientific American, 233(5), 110–12.

Heyes, C.M. (1998) Theory of mind in nonhuman primates. Behavioral and Brain Sciences 21, 101-48; with commentaries.

Heyes, C.M. and Galef, B.G. (eds) (1996) Social Learning in Animals: The Roots of Culture. San Diego, CA, Academic Press.

Hilgard, E.R. (1986) Divided Consciousness: Multiple Controls in Human Thought and Action. New York, Wiley.

Hilton, E.N., Lundberg, T.R. Transgender Women in the Female

Category of Sport: Perspectives on Testosterone Suppression and Performance Advantage. Sports Med 51, 199–214 (2021).

Hitler, Adolf. Mein Kampf, 1925

Holt, J. (1999) Blindsight in debates about qualia. Journal of Consciousness Studies 6(5), 54-71.

Holloway RL (1996) Evolution of the human brain. In: Lock A, Peters CR (eds) Handbook of human symbolic evolution. Oxford University Press, Oxford

Jackson, F. (1982) Epiphenomenal qualia. Philosophical Quarterly 32, 127-36.

James, W. (1890) The Principles of Psychology (2 volumes). London, Macmillan.

James, W. (1902) The Varieties of Religious Experience: A Study in

Human Nature. New York and London, Longmans, Green and Co.

Jay, M. (ed.) (1999) Artificial Paradises: A Drugs Reader. London, Penguin.

Jaynes, J. (1976) The Origin of Consciousness in the Breakdown of the Bicameral Mind. New York, Houghton Mifflin.

Johnson, M.K. and Raye, C.L. (1981) Reality monitoring. Psychological Review 88, 67-85.

Kadim I, Mahgoub O, Baqir S et al. (2015) Cultured meat from muscle stem cells: a review of challenges and prospects. J Integr Agr 14: 222–233

Kandel, E. R. In Search of Memory: The Emergence of a New Science of Mind, W. W. Norton & Company (2007).

Kandel E. R. Schwartz JH, Jessel TM. Principles of neural sciences. New York; McGraw Hill, 2000.

Kihlstrom, J.F. (1996) Perception without awareness of what is perceived, learning without awareness of what is learned. In M. Velmans (ed.) The Science of Consciousness. London, Routledge, 23-46.

Kjaer, Troels, Camilla Bertelsen, Paola Piccini, David Brooks, Jorgen Alving, and Hans Lou. "Increased Dopamine Tone during Meditation- Induced Change of Consciousness." Cognitive Brain Research 13, no. 2 (April 2002)

Kölmel HW. 1985. Complex visual hallucinations in the hemianopic field. J Neurol Neurosurg Psychiatry.

Koenig, Harold. "Research on Religion, Spirituality, and Mental Health: A Review." Canadian Journal of Psychiatry 54, no. 5 (May 2009)

Koenig, Harold, ed. Handbook of Religion and Mental Health. San Diego, CA: Academic Press, 1998

Kraepelin E. Psychiatry: A Textbook for Students and Physicians. New York, NY: Science History Publications; 1990.

Lauglin, Charles, John McManus, and Eugene d'Aquili. Brain, Symbol, and Experience. 2nd ed. New York: Columbia University Press, 1992

LeDoux, J. E. (1996). The emotional brain. New York: Simon & Schuster.

LeDoux, J.E. (1992), 'Emotion and the amygdala', in The Amygdala: Neurobiological Aspects of Emo- tion, Memory and Mental Dysfunction, ed J.P. Aggleton (New York: Wiley-Liss).

Levin, D.T. and Simons, D.J. (1997) Failure to detect changes to attended objects in motion pictures. Psychonomic Bulletin and Review 4, 501-6.

Levine,J. (1983) Materialism and qualia: the explanatory gap. Pacific Philosophical Quarterly 64, 354-61.

Lewicki, P., Czyzewska, M. and Hoffman, H. (1987) Unconscious acquisition of complex procedural knowledge. Journal of Experimental Psychology: Learning, Memory and Cognition 13, 523-30.

Lewicki, P., Hill, T. and Czyzewska, M. (1992) Nonconscious acquisition of information. American Psychologist 47, 796-801.

Naskar, Abhijit. "Homo: A Brief History of Consciousness", 2015

Naskar, Abhijit. "What is Mind?", 2016

Naskar, Abhijit. "Love, God & Neurons: Memoir of A Scientist who found himself by getting lost", 2016

Naskar, Abhijit. "Principia Humanitas", 2017

Naskar, Abhijit. "We Are All Black: A Treatise on Racism", 2017

Naskar, Abhijit. "Either Civilized or Phobic: A Treatise on Homosexuality", 2017

Naskar, Abhijit. "The Bengal Tigress: A Treatise on Gender Equality", 2017

Naskar, Abhijit. "Morality Absolute", 2017

Naskar, Abhijit. "Build Bridges not Walls: In the name of Americana", 2018

Naskar, Abhijit. "Fabric of Humanity", 2018

Naskar, Abhijit. "Citizens of Peace: Beyond the Savagery of Sovereignty", 2019

Naskar, Abhijit. "The Constitution of The United Peoples of Earth", 2019

Naskar, Abhijit. "Neurons Giveth, Neurons Taketh Away | Abhijit Naskar | TEDxIIMRanchi", 2019 https://www.youtube.com/watch?v=B NX-Q0ySm80

Naskar, Abhijit. "Mission Reality", 2019

Naskar, Abhijit. "Operation Justice: To Make A Society That Needs No Law", 2019

Naskar, Abhijit. "Every Generation Needs Caretakers: The Gospel of Patriotism", 2020

Naskar, Abhijit. "Hurricane Humans: Give me accountability, I'll give you peace", 2020

Naskar, Abhijit. "Revolution Indomable", 2020

Naskar, Abhijit. "Servitude is Sanctitude", 2020

Naskar, Abhijit. "Good Scientist: When Science and Service Combine", 2020

Newberg, Andrew. "How God Changes Your Brain: An Introduction to Jewish Neurotheology", CCAR Journal: The Reform Jewish Quarterly, Winter 2016.

Newberg, Andrew, and Stephanie Newberg. "A Neuropsychological Perspective on Spiritual Development." In Handbook of Spiritual Development in Childhood and Adolescence, edited by Eugene Roehlkepartain, Pamela King, Linda Wagener, and Peter Benson. London: Sage Publications, Inc., 2005

Newberg, Andrew. "The Neurotheology Link An Intersection Between Spirituality and Health", Alternative and Complimentary Therapies, Vol 21 No 1, February 2015.

Newberg, Andrew, Nancy Wintering, Dharma Khalsa, Hannah Roggenkamp, and Mark Waldman. "Meditation Effects on Cognitive Function and Cerebral Blood Flow in Subjects with Memory Loss: A Preliminary Study." Journal of Alzheimer's Disease 20, no. 2 (2010)

Nash, M. (1995), 'Glimpses of the mind', Time.

Nesse RM. Proximate and evolutionary studies of anxiety, stress and depression: synergy at the interface. Neurosci Biobehav Rev. 1999;23:895-903.

Nicolelis, Miguel. (2011) "Beyond Boundaries: The New Neuroscience of Connecting Brains with Machines--- and How It Will Change Our Lives", Times Books

O'Hara, K. and Scutt, T. (1996) There is no hard problem of consciousness. Journal of Consciousness Studies 3(4), 290-302, reprinted in J. Shear (ed.) (1997) Explaining Consciousness. Cambridge, MA, MIT Press, 69-82.

Penrose, R. (1994), Shadows of the Mind (Oxford: Oxford University Press).

Penrose, R. (1989), The Emperor's New Mind: Concerning Computers, Minds and The Laws of Physics (Oxford: Oxford University Press).

Persinger, "'I would kill in God's name' role of sex, weekly church attendance, report of a religious experience and limbic lability" Perceptual and Motor Skills 1997.

Persinger "Experimental simulation of the God experience" Neurotheology 2003.

Persinger, Corradini, Clement, Keaney, et al "Neurotheology and its convergence with neuroquantology" NeuroQuantology 2010.

Persinger, Koren and St-Pierre "The electromagnetic induction of mystical and altered states within the laboratory" Journal of Consciousness Exploration and Research 2010.

Persinger "Case report: A prototypical spontaneous 'sensed presence' of a sentient being and concomitant electroencephalographic activity in the clinical laboratory" Neurocase 2008.

Persinger and Saroka "Potential production of Hughlings Jackson's "parasitic consciousness" by physiologically-patterned weak transcerebral magnetic fields: QEEG and source localization" Epilepsy & Behavior 28 (2013).

Persinger. "The neuropsychiatry of paranormal experiences". J Neuropsychiatry Clin Neurosci 2001.

Persinger. "Neuropsychological bases of god beliefs", New York: Praeger, 1987

Persinger. "Temporal lobe epileptic signs and correlative behaviors displayed by normal populations", Journal of General Psychology, 1986

Perry BD, Pollard R. Homeostasis, stress, trauma, and adaptation. A neurodevelopmental view of childhood trauma. Child Adolesc Psychiatr Clin N Am. 1998;7:33.

Puce A, Perrett D (2003) Electrophysiological and brain imaging of biological motion. Philosoph Trans Royal Soc Lond, Series B, 358: 435–445.

Ramachandran VS. Behavioral and magnetoencephalographic correlates of plasticity in the adult human brain. Proc Natl Acad Sci USA 1993; 90: 10413–20.

Ramachandran VS. Phantom limbs, neglect syndromes, repressed memories, and Freudian psychology. Int Rev Neurobiol 1994; 37: 291–333.

Ramachandran VS. Plasticity and functional recovery in neurology. Clin Med 2005; 5: 368–73.

Ramachandran VS, Hirstein W. The perception of phantom limbs. The D. O. Hebb lecture. Brain 1998; 121: 1603–30.

Ramachandran VS, Rogers-Ramachandran D, Cobb S. Touching

the phantom limb. Nature 1995; 377: 489–90.

Ramachandran VS, Rogers-Ramachandran D. Phantom limbs and neural plasticity. Arch Neurol 2000; 57: 317–20.

Ramachandran VS, Rogers-Ramachandran D. It's all done with mirrors. Sci Am Mind 2007; 18: 16–9.

Ramachandran VS, Rogers-Ramachandran D. Sensations referred to a patient's phantom arm from another subjects intact arm: perceptual correlates of mirror neurons. Med Hypotheses 2008; 70: 1233–4.

Ramachandran VS, Rogers-Ramachandran D, Stewart M. Perceptual correlates of massive cortical reorganization. Science 1992; 258: 1159–60.

Rizzolatti G, Craighero L (2004) The mirror-neuron system. Annu Rev Neurosci 27: 169–192.

Rose'n B, Lundborg G. Training with a mirror in rehabilitation of the hand. Scand J Plast Reconstr Surg Hand Surg 2005; 39: 104–8.

Roberts, TA; Smalley, J; Ahrendt, D (December 2020). "Effect of gender affirming hormones on athletic performance in transwomen and transmen: implications for sporting organisations and legislators". British Journal of Sports Medicine. 55 (11): 577–583

Rozin R Haidt J and McCauley CR (2000) Disgust. In: Lewis M, Haviland-Jones JM (eds) Handbook of Emotion. 2nd Edition. Guilford Press, New York, pp 637–653.

Saxe R, Carey S, Kanwisher N (2004) Understanding other minds: linking developmental psychology and functional neuroimaging. Annu Rev Psychol 55: 87–124.

S. J. Russell and P. Norvig, Artificial intelligence: a modern approach (3rd edition): Prentice Hall, 2009.

Smith A (1759) The theory of moral sentiments (ed. 1976). Clarendon Press, Oxford.

Schilling, Vincent. 2017, indian country today

Stein, Stephen K. 2017, The Sea in World History: Exploration, Travel, and Trade

Tesla N. "My Inventions", 1919